Juices for Triathletes

The Recipes, Nutrition and Diet Solution for Maximum Endurance and Improved Training Results for Sprint through to Ironman Distance Triathlons (Food for Fitness Series)

Lars Andersen

Published by Nordic Standard Publishing

Atlanta, Georgia USA

ISBN 978-1-484145-18-0

Lars Andersen

What Our Readers Are Saying

"Really useful guide with everything you need to know about nutrition for the sport"

★★★★☆ **Alanna J. Sais (Mount Eden, KY)**

"These recipes are so quick and easy that I get to spend more time training and less time in the kitchen - awesome!"

★★★★☆ **Chanell C. Bergeron (Lakeland, FL)**

"I was expecting just another recipe book but was pleasantly surprised by the amount of useful information, tips and tricks contained within"

★★★★★ **Leora J. Miner (Newark, AR)**

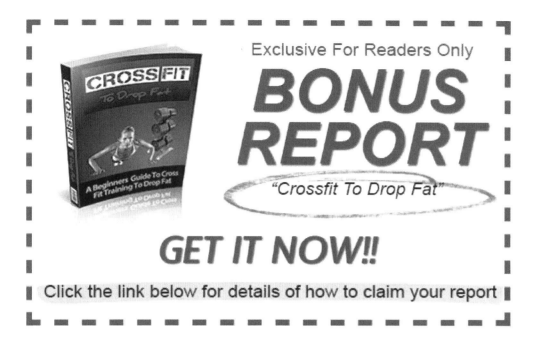

Exclusive Bonus Download: Crossfit to Drop Fat

CrossFit is the principal strength and conditioning program for many police academies and tactical operations teams, military special operations units, champion martial artists, and hundreds of other elite and professional athletes worldwide.

Inside this ebook you will learn:

- The history of Cross fit training
- What is Cross fit training
- Advice on how to live life to the fullest yet still shred pounds
- Practical advice on the best exercises for cross fit
- The benefits of cross fit training
- Tips to help you succeed
- and more...

Go to the end of this book for the download link for this Bonus!

Thank you for downloading my book. Please REVIEW this book on Amazon. I need your feedback to make the next edition better. Thank you so much!

Books by Lars Andersen

The Smoothies for Runners Book

Juices for Runners

Smoothies for Cyclists

Juices for Cyclists

Paleo Diet for Cyclists

Smoothies for Triathletes

Juices for Triathletes

Paleo Diet for Triathletes

Smoothies for Strength

Juices for Strength

Paleo Diet for Strength

Paleo Diet Smoothies for Strength

Smoothies for Golfers

Juices for Golfers

Table of Contents

Disclaimer

Juices and Juicing for Triathletes

"Tell me what you eat, and I will tell you who you are" - Brillat-Savarin

If you take part in triathlon events, you need energy ... and lots of it! The foods you eat on a daily basis are your·body's only source of energy so whether you compete in sprint distance, Olympic distance, long-distance or Ironman events, consuming a balanced diet of quality nutrients is essential to fuel your performance.

Juicing is a fast and efficient way to maximize your nutrient intake. A fresh juice every morning before a training session is a great way to energize your body without overloading your stomach with heavy foods that might lead to discomfort as you exercise. The nutrients contained in juiced fruits and vegetables are readily absorbed by your body as the insoluble fiber that slows digestion is removed in the juicing process. In this "pre-digested" form, the health-boosting vitamin and mineral content is effectively "unlocked" and can therefore be of maximum benefit to your body.

Fruits and vegetables provide energy to fuel your training, whether swimming, cycling or running, and they are also packed with vitamins, minerals and antioxidants which help to give your immune system a boost. Many varieties also contain anti-inflammatory properties which aid your body's recovery process after a hard or prolonged effort. Just as a car engine needs quality fuel to perform at its best, your body also needs quality fuel to give a quality performance. A delicious, nutritious juice is a convenient way to provide premium fuel for your body.

Tanking Up

The key to getting the most from a juice is to use a juicing machine that allows the maximum nutrition to be extracted from the fruits and vegetables you choose. A quality juicer not only extracts the juice from the flesh but also from the peelings, seeds and pits. Not all juicers are suitable for all fruits - citrus fruits require a citrus juicer for example - so it's important to consider the type of produce you want to juice to ensure you get the best machine for your needs. Machines which limit the amount of heat generated in the juicing process also help to maximize the nutritional content by preserving the live enzyme content and antioxidant benefits. Raw fruit and vegetable juices contain enzymes that help your body to convert food into energy. All of your body's metabolic processes, including the conversion of foods into fuel, generate the formation of free radicals. These are chemicals which can be harmful to your health if left unchecked. Antioxidants protect your body against free radicals and they are abundant in a huge variety of fruits and vegetables. This makes a fresh juice a great pre-training source of health-boosting energy and also a post-training source of vital nutrients to help your body recover, regenerate and refuel in preparation for your next training session or event.

The longer the duration or the greater the intensity of your training sessions, the more energy your body needs to keep going. A balanced, energy-providing diet contains a healthy mix of carbohydrates, fats, protein, vitamins and minerals.

Carbohydrates

Carbohydrates are described as "the athlete's best friend" as they provide the main source of energy to fuel performance. They can be split into two categories:

Simple carbohydrates - sources include:

Sugary foodstuffs such as candy, cakes and sodas

Honey, in the form of glucose

Fruits and vegetables, in the form fructose and sucrose

Milk and dairy products, in the form of lactose

Malted wheat and barley, sprouting grains and malt extract, in the form of maltose

Molasses, dextrose, corn syrup and invert syrup.

Simple carbohydrates or **sugars** provide a fast-acting, virtually "instant" source of energy.

Complex carbohydrates - sources include:

Starchy foods such as bread and potatoes

Cereals

Pasta

Complex carbohydrates or **starch** provide a relatively slow-acting, steady source of energy. **Fiber** is also a complex carbohydrate, providing a steady source of energy with the added benefit of promoting regular, healthy bowel movements. The fiber content of fruits and vegetables helps to slow the energy release from the natural sugars, thereby helping to keep you healthfully energized for longer. Fiber can be further categorized as insoluble or soluble. Insoluble fiber is found in the skins of many fruits and vegetables, therefore the juicing process removes this form in most cases. Soluble fiber is found in the flesh of a variety of fruits and in some vegetables, therefore it remains present in most juices. Juicing fruits and vegetables gives your body a break from the process of digesting insoluble fiber. With the fiber removed, only water, vitamins and minerals remain, allowing for a much faster uptake of nutrients.

All forms of carbohydrate are broken down into glucose and glycogen before they can be used. Complex carbohydrates are broken down more slowly than simple carbohydrates, resulting in a slower release of energy, but honey is the only simple carbohydrate that can be used by your body straight away. Glucose and glycogen are your body's source of fuel for everyday activities as well as for training and competing and they are inter-convertible. When you have a sufficient supply of glucose, your body stores any excess carbohydrates in the form of glycogen in your liver and muscles. If the supply of glucose then falls short of the energy demand, your body converts the stored glycogen into glucose ready for use.

One gram of carbohydrate provides four calories. However, your body can only store a limited amount of glycogen, with the muscles able to store enough for up to around two hours of intense exercise. After exercising, your body's ability to store glycogen is elevated. This period of around 30 minutes is known as the "glycogen window" and consuming appropriate foods in this window helps replenish glycogen stores, promote muscle repair and restoration, and thereby aid recovery after a long or intense training session or event.

Fats

Fats also provide energy with one gram of fat providing nine calories. They act as a carrier for fat-soluble vitamins, including vitamins A, D, K, and E, they provide insulation for your body, and they protect vital organs. Your body can make its own fat from excess carbohydrates and protein in your diet but it cannot manufacture certain essential unsaturated fats, meaning that the foods you eat are your body's only supply. The essential fatty acids are **omega-3** and **omega-6**.

Many athletes avoid fat in their diet, believing it to be unhealthy, but not allfats are equal and "healthy" fat is an essential element of a balanced diet.

Healthy fats:

Monounsaturated fatty acids - sources include olive oil, rapeseed oil, avocados, nuts and seeds.

Polyunsaturated fatty acids - sources include most vegetable oils, fish oils and oily fish. These also contain the essential fatty acids omega-6 and omega-3. Good sources of omega-6 include olive oil and sunflower oil. Good sources of omega-3 include green leafy vegetables, soya bean oil, rapeseed oil, walnuts, linseed or flax seeds and oily fish such as sardines, salmon and mackerel.

The average Western individual has around 60 times more energy stored in their body as fat than energy stored as glycogen in the liver and muscles. During endurance sports such as triathlon, the body conserves as much of its glycogen reserves as possible by using some of its fat stores for energy. However, compared to carbohydrate, fat is a very slow source of energy, meaning that as the intensity of the exercise increases, the body switches to using glycogen to provide a faster release of energy. One potential bonus of fat consumption for athletes is that it provides over twice the calories of carbohydrate, weight for weight, without creating too much bulk in the stomach.

Protein

Protein is essentially the body's muscle-builder but it is only used as a source of energy if your body's glycogen stores have been depleted. However, protein is of particular value to triathletes and endurance athletes as it plays an important role in repairing the muscles that may suffer damage through repetitive wear and tear.

The Benefits of a Pre-training Juice

Fruits and vegetables contain carbohydrates, making them a nutritious way to top up your glycogen stores before a training session. They are also a rich source of vitamins, minerals and antioxidants, making them extremely important in terms of promoting and maintaining optimum health. Any combination of juiced fruits will provide energy-giving carbohydrates so your choice is a matter of personal taste. The antioxidant properties of many fruits can also help to reduce the effects of muscular damage generated through training. Vitamin C, vitamin E, and beta-carotene are particularly effective at limiting the potentially damaging effects of free radicals.

Popular juicing fruits include:

Grapefruit - a rich source of vitamin C and a good source of pectin which provides fiber.

Apples - a good source of vitamin C, bioflavonoids and soluble fiber. Bioflavonoids are powerful antioxidants.

Pears - a good source of vitamin C, potassium, bioflavonoids and pectin. Potassium is essential for the transmission of all nerve impulses.

Kiwi fruit - a rich source of vitamin C and a good source of potassium.

Cherries - a good source of potassium and a useful source of vitamin C. On-going research has found that cherry juice contains anti-inflammatory properties which may be of additional benefit to endurance athletes. A study involving marathon runners concluded that those who drank cherry juice recovered faster after training than those who did not. The antioxidant content helps to reduce inflammation, thereby helping to promote faster muscle recovery.

Apricots - a rich source of beta-carotene, the plant form of vitamin A which helps to protect against free radicals, and vitamin C.

Watermelon - contains vitamin C and potassium which works in tandem with sodium to help regulate the body's fluid balance.

Blueberries - contain as much as five times more antioxidant properties than other fruits! When blueberries are out of season, frozen varieties provide a useful alternative, or cranberries, grapes, blackberries and goji berries all make good substitutes.

As a general guide, fruits with orange or dark yellow flesh provide a good source of beta-carotene, and fruits with red flesh offer a good source of lycopene. The combination of beta-carotene and lycopene is thought to be very effective in terms of protecting your body against free radicals.

The water content of fruits varies. The higher the water content, the easier a fruit is to juice. The lower the water content, the more likely it is that blending will yield a better end result than juicing. Adding blended fruits to a juice, or putting back some of the pulp created in the juicing process, is a tasty way to thicken the consistency of a juice and increase the fiber content if desired. Fruits suitable for blending include:

Strawberries- a rich source of vitamin C and also an aid to the absorption of iron from vegetables. Iron is essential for the production of hemoglobin, the oxygen carrying pigment found in red blood cells.

Bananas - a rich source of potassium.

Avocados - a rich source of vitamin E and a good source of potassium. Avocados also have a high "healthy" fat content and can contain as many as 400 calories per fruit!

"Hobby" triathletes training for short-distance events will generally find that a simple juice containing just one or two fruits will satisfy their needs by providing an energizing pre-training boost. However, triathletes training more intensely with the goal of improving overall performance will benefit from the addition of extra carbohydrates. As a general rule, you should add 0.45 grams of carbohydrate per each pound of body weight before a moderate intensity session of two to four hours and 0.68 grams of carbohydrates per pound of body weight before an intense session of four or more hours.

As an example, two tablespoons of honey provides 50 grams of carbohydrate. Honey contains glucose which is an instantly useable source of energy. One large mango also provides 50 grams of carbohydrates, and three or four apples or pears will provide the same. Another way to increase the carbohydrate content by 50 grams and slow the release of energy before a longer duration training session is to add two blended bananas, one avocado, or one small pot of yogurt to your fruit juice.

Vegetables also offer a healthful source of carbohydrates for energy and many vegetables contain health boosting vitamin, mineral and antioxidant properties along with plant protein. Green fruits and vegetables contain chlorophyll which has been shown to stimulate the production of hemoglobin. This can lead to improvements in your oxygen uptake and your body's ability to utilize it, referred to as your VO2 max, as well as giving your overall energy levels a boost. This is great news for competitive triathletes as improvements in VO2 max can lead to significant improvements in race times. A nutritious green juice can be made with green leafy vegetables; cruciferous vegetables, including broccoli, cauliflower and cabbage; grasses, including wheat grass and barley grass; algae, including chlorella and spirulina (also available in powder form); vegetable sprouts and sea vegetables. Most green vegetables are naturally alkaline which provides an additional benefit to triathletes. One cause of muscle fatigue in endurance events is the elevation of acidity levels in your blood. Regularly consuming green vegetables helps to regulate and minimize the acidity of your blood and thereby improve your performance by allowing you to train for longer without fatigue. A green juice is an extremely efficient way to gain the full benefit of "getting your greens" on a daily basis!

Popular juicing vegetables include:

Carrot - a rich source of beta-carotene.

Beets - a rich source of nutrients, including folate, an essential vitamin for cell health, potassium and vitamin C. The leafy tops contain beta-carotene, calcium and iron. Research has also found that drinking juiced beets on a regular basis can enhance an athlete's tolerance to high-intensity exercise, making beet juice a popular choice for triathletes and long-distance runners and cyclists.

Celery - a good source of potassium.

Romaine Lettuce - a useful source of folate and beta-carotene

Cauliflower - a good source of vitamin C.

Cabbage - a rich source of vitamin C, vitamin K, and a good source of vitamin E, potassium and beta-carotene. Vitamin K is essential in the formation of many proteins.

Broccoli - another rich source of vitamin C. Broccoli also contains beta-carotene, iron and potassium, and is high in bioflavonoids and other antioxidants.

Pumpkin - a good source of beta-carotene and vitamin E. Pumpkin seeds are rich in iron, phosphorus, potassium, magnesium and zinc. Pumpkin juice is a favorite among Harry Potter fans!

Spinach - a rich source of carotenoids, including beta-carotene and lutein, which are powerful antioxidants. Also contains vitamin C and potassium.

Collard Greens - a good source of omega-3 essential fatty acids which have anti-inflammatory properties.

Kale - a good source of iron, calcium, vitamin C and beta-carotene.

Fennel - contains beta-carotene and folate, but particularly useful for adding flavor.

Watercress - contains vitamin C, beta-carotene and iron, and is also 91 percent water.

The Benefits of Post-training Juice

The plant proteins contained in vegetables help to promote healthy tissue growth and repair, making them of particular benefit after long or intense training sessions that may lead to muscle damage. A juice containing a flavorsome mix of fruits and vegetables consumed within the 30 minute post-training glycogen window is an effective way to help your body recover after your efforts and also replenish depleted glycogen stores so that you'll be fully energized for your next training effort or event. During this window, the enzymes in your body responsible for making glycogen are more active, meaning that glycogen stores can be replenished faster by consuming carbohydrate-rich foods. The plant protein contained in vegetables promotes muscle repair and regeneration after a hard effort and also stimulates the action of insulin which boosts glycogen replacement by aiding the transportation of glucose from the blood to the muscles.

Restoring your body's electrolyte balance is an important element of recovery after a long or intense training session. Electrolytes are particles that circulate in your blood and help to regulate your body's fluid balance. An intense swim, cycle or run session can lead to muscle soreness and inflammation but a post-training juice can help to minimize the damage and speed the recovery process.

Hydration

Adequate hydration is essential at all times and of particular importance to long-distance triathletes. Fluids must be carried with you on your bike ride and also on your run so that small, frequent sips can be taken to help maintain hydration levels. Hydration levels can be boosted before a training session by drinking a large glass of water and replaced after a session in the same way, but a fresh juice provides a practical way to boost your fluid *and* nutrient intakewithout overloading your stomach and potentially causing discomfort.

Remaining hydrated during a training session or race is essential as fluid in your blood transports glucose to the working muscles and takes away the metabolic by-products. A fresh juice provides a practical way to top up and replenish essential fluids but it's worth noting that the water content of the fruits or vegetables you choose can significantly increase your overall fluid intake.

The water content of fruits and vegetables:

Cucumber - 96 percent water

Lettuce - 96 percent water

Celery - 95 percent water

Zucchini - 95 percent water

Melon - 94 percent water

Red tomatoes - 94 percent water

Cabbage - 93 percent water

Grapefruit - 91 percent water

Watercress - 91 percent water

Strawberries - 89 percent water

Carrots - 87 percent water

Oranges - 86 percent water

Peaches - 86 percent water

Apples - 84 percent water

Grapes - 79 percent water

Tasty Flavor Combinations

Combining fruits and vegetables is a delicious way to get the maximum nutritional benefit from a juice. Fruits add sweetness which can make a green juice more palatable, but other great ways to add flavor and interest include:

Ginger - research has found that ginger can be helpful in reducing muscle aches after intense exercise.

Garlic - contains antiviral and antibacterial properties.

Parsley - one cup of parsley contains 2 grams of protein. It is also rich in calcium and provides iron, copper, magnesium, potassium, zinc, phosphorus, beta-carotene and vitamin C.

Dill – adds a sweet flavor to a vegetable juice and contains calcium, iron, manganese, vitamin C, and beta-carotene.

Sorrel - provides iron, magnesium and calcium.

Basil - provides beta-carotene, iron, potassium, copper, manganese and magnesium.

Coriander - provides a mild, peppery flavor along with anti-inflammatory properties, vitamin C, iron and magnesium.

Turmeric - contains antibacterial, antibiotic and anti-inflammatory properties. It also adds a vibrant yellow color!

Nutmeg - adds richness and warmth to any vegetable juice. Works particularly well with cauliflower.

Cayenne - a rich source of vitamin A.

Black pepper - contains iron, beta-carotene, vitamin C and bioflavonoids.

Fresh ginger, garlic and parsley can all be juiced along with fruits and vegetables but dried versions can also be mixed in to "spice up" your juices and add to the nutritional content. Experimentation is the only way to discover the flavor combinations that work best for you. The fresher your ingredients, the more nutritional value they hold, but it is worth noting that frozen produce can represent a good choice when fresh foods may have spent a little longer than ideal on the grocery store shelf. Organic produce will generally offer a healthier choice in terms of the number of chemicals used in the farming process but non-organic produce still provides the nutrients you need to fuel your body and to boost your overall health.

Healthy fat can be added to a juice in the form of extra virgin coconut oil – or any other oil containing essential fatty acids that suits your taste – to provide an extra source of energy-giving calories and anti-inflammatory properties. Coconut oil is in fact a source of saturated fat which is generally considered to be an "unhealthy" source of fat, however, on-going research into the health benefits of consuming coconuts has found that it may be of particular benefit to athletes as it helps to support the immune system and promote healthy tissue growth and repair. The addition of coconut oil to a juice may be of particular benefit to triathletes training and competing in longer distance events as it is utilized by the body as a source of energy in preference to being stored as fat.

Variety is the spice of life, and this is certainly true when it comes to mixing up juices. The more variety and color you have in your diet, the more nutritionally beneficial it's likely to be. Colorful combinations include:

Beets and carrot

Apple and grape

Carrot and mango

Kale and kiwi fruit

Red cabbage and pear

Using tried-and-tested juice recipes is a great way to get started as they take all of the guess work out of finding the best flavor combinations. However, you will soon discover the combinations that please your taste-buds the most and those that provide you with the biggest boost in your energy levels. A daily juice does not only taste great, it makes you feel great. There's a saying, "The proof of the pudding is in the tasting," and this can also be applied to juicing. The proof of the juice is not only in the tasting, but also in the energizing!

General Information about Your Juices

These juices are divided into 3 categories, each designed to meet the nutritional needs of the triathlete at three key moments:

Pre-competition – for competitions/workouts lasting 2 to 4 hours;

Pre-competition – for high competitions/ workouts lasting 4 or more hours;

Post-competition.

The great majority of the ingredients in these recipes have a low Glycemic Index.

If you can't find the fresh fruit you need for a recipe, feel free to replace it with frozen. Frozen fruits have the same nutritional content as the corresponding fresh fruits.

You can adjust the consistency of your juice adding some ice cubes to the recipe before blending and/or straining before serving.

If you are looking for new flavors, try replacing ice the ice cubes in the recipes for frozen cubes of your favorite tea.

Pre-Competition Juices – for Competitions/Workouts Lasting 2 to 4 Hours

These juices were developed to provide an adequate amount of Carbohydrates to a 150 pounds person. You can adjust the amount of carbohydrates by adding one of the following by each extra 5 pounds of body weight:

- ½ tsp. of honey;
- 1 tbsp. of flax seed;
- ¼ tbsp. of fruit jam;
- 1 tsp. of seeded raisins;
- ½ tbsp. of dried apricots;
- 3 ½ tbsps. of reduced fat milk;
- 2 ½ tbsps. of low fat yogurt.

1. Papaya and Blueberries Juice

Preparation time	5 minutes
Ready time	5 minutes
Serves	1
Serving quantity/unit	600 G / 21 Ounces
Calories	272 Cal
Total Fat	1g
Cholesterol	0 mg
Sodium	13 mg
Total Carbohydrates	69 g
Dietary fibers	12 g
Sugars	44 g
Protein	4 g

Prepare your juice combining the following ingredients in a juicer/food processor:

- 2 ½ cups of papaya
- 1 ½ cups of blueberries
- ¼ cup of strawberries

2. Passion Fruit and Apple Juice with Cauliflower

Preparation time	5 minutes
Ready time	5 minutes
Serves	1
Serving quantity/unit	500 G / 18 Ounces
Calories	270 Cal
Total Fat	1 g
Cholesterol	0 mg
Sodium	53 mg
Total Carbohydrates	68 g
Dietary fibers	20 g
Sugars	43 g
Protein	4 g

Prepare your juice combining the following ingredients in a juicer/food processor:

- ½ cup of passion fruit
- 2 ½ cups of chopped apple
- ½ cup of cauliflower
- 3 ice cubes

3. Loquat and Orange Juice

Preparation time	5 minutes
Ready time	5 minutes
Serves	1
Serving quantity/unit	650 G / 18 Ounces
Calories	294 Cal
Total Fat	1g
Cholesterol	0 mg
Sodium	7 mg
Total Carbohydrates	70 g
Dietary fibers	4 g
Sugars	42 g
Protein	4 g

Prepare your juice combining the following ingredients in a juicer/food processor:

- 2 cups of fresh orange juice
- 1 cup of loquat
- 1 tsp. of mint

4. Pear and Lemon Juice

Preparation time	5 minutes
Ready time	5 minutes
Serves	1
Serving quantity/unit	475 G / 17 Ounces
Calories	252 Cal
Total Fat	0 g
Cholesterol	0 mg
Sodium	6 mg
Total Carbohydrates	68 g
Dietary fibers	11 g
Sugars	45 g
Protein	2 g

Prepare your juice combining the following ingredients in a juicer/food processor:

- 2 ¼ cups of sliced pear
- 2 ½ tbsps. of lemon juice
- 1 ½ tsps. of honey
- 3 ice cubes

5. Pineapple and Apple Juice

Preparation time	5 minutes
Ready time	5 minutes
Serves	1
Serving quantity/unit	580 G / 17 Ounces
Calories	260 Cal
Total Fat	1 g
Cholesterol	0 mg
Sodium	7 mg
Total Carbohydrates	69 g
Dietary fibers	9 g
Sugars	52 g
Protein	2g

Prepare your juice combining the following ingredients in a juicer/food processor:

- 2 ¼ cups of pineapple
- 1 ½ cups of chopped apple
- 3 ice cubes

6. Grape and Melon Juice

Preparation time	5 minutes
Ready time	5 minutes
Serves	1
Serving quantity/unit	650 G / 17 Ounces
Calories	282 Cal
Total Fat	2 g
Cholesterol	0 mg
Sodium	79 mg
Total Carbohydrates	70 g
Dietary fibers	6g
Sugars	67 g
Protein	5g

Prepare your juice combining the following ingredients in a juicer/food processor:

- 2 cups of grapes
- 3 cups of cubed melon

7. Apple, Papaya and Watermelon Juice

Preparation time	5 minutes
Ready time	5 minutes
Serves	1
Serving quantity/unit	600 G / 21 Ounces
Calories	262 Cal
Total Fat	1 g
Cholesterol	0 mg
Sodium	12 mg
Total Carbohydrates	68 g
Dietary fibers	10 g
Sugars	49 g
Protein	3 g

Prepare your juice combining the following ingredients in a juicer/food processor:

- 1 ½ cups of chopped apple
- 1 cup of cubed watermelon
- 2 cups of papaya
- 1 tsp. of honey

8. Peach and Loquats Juice

Preparation time	5 minutes
Ready time	5 minutes
Serves	1
Serving quantity/unit	570 G / 20 Ounces
Calories	270 Cal
Total Fat	1 g
Cholesterol	0 mg
Sodium	3 mg
Total Carbohydrates	68 g
Dietary fibers	9 g
Sugars	37 g
Protein	4 g

Prepare your juice combining the following ingredients in a juicer/food processor:

- 2 cups of peach
- 1 ½ cups of loquats
- 1 ½ tsps. of honey

9. Fennel and pineapple Juice

Preparation time	5 minutes
Ready time	5 minutes
Serves	1
Serving quantity/unit	500 G / 18 Ounces
Calories	268 Cal
Total Fat	1 g
Cholesterol	0 mg
Sodium	28 mg
Total Carbohydrates	70 g
Dietary fibers	8g
Sugars	52 g
Protein	3g

Prepare your juice combining the following ingredients in a juicer/food processor:

- ½ cup of sliced fennel bulb
- 3 cups of pineapple
- 1 tsp. of honey
- 1 tsp. of mint

10. Banana and Strawberry Juice

Preparation time	5 minutes
Ready time	5 minutes
Serves	1
Serving quantity/unit	440 G / 16 Ounces
Calories	268 Cal
Total Fat	1 g
Cholesterol	0 mg
Sodium	6 mg
Total Carbohydrates	68 g
Dietary fibers	9g
Sugars	40 g
Protein	3g

Prepare your juice combining the following ingredients in a juicer/food processor:

- 1 ½ cups of sliced banana
- 1 cup of strawberry
- 1 tsp. of honey
- 3 ice cubes

11. Mango, Pear and Loquat Juice

Preparation time	5 minutes
Ready time	5 minutes
Serves	1
Serving quantity/unit	450 G / 16 Ounces
Calories	259 Cal
Total Fat	1g
Cholesterol	0 mg
Sodium	6 mg
Total Carbohydrates	68 g
Dietary fibers	11 g
Sugars	44 g
Protein	2 g

Prepare your juice combining the following ingredients in a juicer/food processor:

- 1 ¼ cups of sliced pear
- 1 cup of mango
- ½ cup of loquat

Pre-Competition Juices- for Competitions/Workouts Lasting 4 or More Hours

Like the previous juices, these are also designed to provide an adequate amount of Carbohydrates to a 150 pounds person. Nothing to worry about if you weigh less than 150 pounds, but if you weight more than this, consider adjusting the amount of carbohydrates by adding one of the following by each extra 5 pounds of your body weight.

- ¾ tsp. of honey;
- 1 ½ tbsps. of flax seed;
- 1 tsp. of fruit jam;
- 1 ½ tsps. of seeded raisins;
- 1 tbsp. of dried apricots;
- 5 tbsps. of reduced fat milk;
- 3 tbsps. of low fat yogurt.

12. Coconut and Passion fruit Juice

Preparation time	5 minutes
Ready time	5 minutes
Serves	1
Serving quantity/unit	500 G / 18 Ounces
Calories	542 Cal
Total Fat	16g
Cholesterol	0 mg
Sodium	125mg
Total Carbohydrates	103 g
Dietary fibers	47g
Sugars	49 g
Protein	10g

Prepare your juice combining the following ingredients in a juicer/food processor:

- ½ cup of coconut
- 1 ¾ cups of passion fruit
- 2 ice cubes

13. Pitaya, Kiwi and Cherry Juice

Preparation time	5 minutes
Ready time	5 minutes
Serves	1
Serving quantity/unit	500 G / 18 Ounces
Calories	442 Cal
Total Fat	1g
Cholesterol	0 mg
Sodium	45 mg
Total Carbohydrates	105 g
Dietary fibers	20g
Sugars	71 g
Protein	4g

Prepare your juice combining the following ingredients in a juicer/food processor:

- 1 cup of pitaya juice
- 1 ¼ cups of kiwi
- 1/3 cup of dried cherries

14. Currant and Plum Juice

Preparation time	5 minutes
Ready time	5 minutes
Serves	1
Serving quantity/unit	600 G / 21 Ounces
Calories	407 Cal
Total Fat	2g
Cholesterol	0 mg
Sodium	7 mg
Total Carbohydrates	103 g
Dietary fibers	16g
Sugars	77 g
Protein	7g

Prepare your juice combining the following ingredients in a juicer/food processor:

- 2 cups of currants
- 2 cups of plums
- ¼ cup of raisins
- 1 tsp. of honey

15. Pomegranate and Pear Juice

Preparation time	5 minutes
Ready time	5 minutes
Serves	1
Serving quantity/unit	700 G / 25 Ounces
Calories	387 Cal
Total Fat	0g
Cholesterol	0 mg
Sodium	5 mg
Total Carbohydrates	102 g
Dietary fibers	12g
Sugars	74 g
Protein	3g

Prepare your juice combining the following ingredients in a juicer/food processor:

- 2 cups of sliced pear
- Seeds of 2 medium pomegranates (around 150g/5 ounces each)
- 3 ice cubes

16. Banana and Raspberry juice

Preparation time	5 minutes
Ready time	5 minutes
Serves	1
Serving quantity/unit	600 G / 21 Ounces
Calories	416 Cal
Total Fat	3 g
Cholesterol	0 mg
Sodium	8 mg
Total Carbohydrates	104 g
Dietary fibers	24g
Sugars	53 g
Protein	6 g

Prepare your juice combining the following ingredients in a juicer/food processor:

- 2 cups of raspberries
- 2 cups of sliced banana
- 1 tsp. of honey
- 3 ice cubes

17. Kiwi and Pear Juice with Celery

Preparation time	5 minutes
Ready time	5 minutes
Serves	1
Serving quantity/unit	490 G / 17 Ounces
Calories	399 Cal
Total Fat	2g
Cholesterol	0mg
Sodium	60mg
Total Carbohydrates	103g
Dietary fibers	18g
Sugars	67 g
Protein	5g

Prepare your juice combining the following ingredients in a juicer/food processor:

- 2 cups of sliced pear
- 1 cup of kiwi
- 3 ½ tbsps. of raisins
- ½ cup of celery

18. Apple and Raisin Juice

Preparation time	5 minutes
Ready time	5 minutes
Serves	1
Serving quantity/unit	443 G / 16 Ounces
Calories	385 Cal
Total Fat	1 g
Cholesterol	0 mg
Sodium	13 mg
Total Carbohydrates	102g
Dietary fibers	10g
Sugars	77g
Protein	3g

Prepare your juice combining the following ingredients in a juicer/food processor:

- 2 ¾ cups of chopped apple
- ½ cup of raisins
- ½ tsp. of honey
- 4 ice cubes

19. Banana and Plum Juice

Preparation time	5 minutes
Ready time	5 minutes
Serves	1
Serving quantity/unit	555 G / 20 Ounces
Calories	402 Cal
Total Fat	2 g
Cholesterol	0 mg
Sodium	3 mg
Total Carbohydrates	103 g
Dietary fibers	11g
Sugars	67g
Protein	5g

Prepare your juice combining the following ingredients in a juicer/food processor:

- 2 cups of sliced banana
- 1 ½ cups of plum
- 1 tsp. of honey

20. Melon, Peach and Apricot Juice

Preparation time	5 minutes
Ready time	5 minutes
Serves	1
Serving quantity/unit	551 G / 19 Ounces
Calories	404 Cal
Total Fat	2 g
Cholesterol	0 mg
Sodium	35 mg
Total Carbohydrates	102 g
Dietary fibers	13 g
Sugars	89 g
Protein	7 g

Prepare your juice combining the following ingredients in a juicer/food processor:

- 1 cup of cubed melon
- 1 ¾ cups of peach
- ¾ cup of dried apricots

21. Cherry, Prune and Cucumber Juice

Preparation time	5 minutes
Ready time	5 minutes
Serves	1
Serving quantity/unit	556 G / 20 Ounces
Calories	410 Cal
Total Fat	1 g
Cholesterol	0 mg
Sodium	5 mg
Total Carbohydrates	105 g
Dietary fibers	13g
Sugars	72g
Protein	6g

Prepare your juice combining the following ingredients in a juicer/food processor:

- 2 ½ cups of cherries
- ½ cup of prunes
- 1 ½ cups of peeled cucumber

Post-Competition Juices

These juices are richer in protein, providing great combinations of carbohydrate and protein which will be essential to give your body the right nutrients, enhancing its recovery after your ride.

22. Peach and cinnamon Juice

Preparation time	5 minutes
Ready time	5 minutes
Serves	1
Serving quantity/unit	530 G / 19 Ounces
Calories	268 Cal
Total Fat	1 g
Cholesterol	0 mg
Sodium	1 mg
Total Carbohydrates	68 g
Dietary fibers	9g
Sugars	60 g
Protein	5g

Prepare your juice combining the following ingredients in a juicer/food processor:

- 3 cups of peach
- ½ cup of tea prepared with one peach flavored tea bag
- 1 tbsp. of honey
- 1 tsp. of cinnamon

23. Loquat and Cherry Juice

Preparation time	5 minutes
Ready time	5 minutes
Serves	1
Serving quantity/unit	450 G / 20 Ounces
Calories	271 Cal
Total Fat	1g
Cholesterol	0 mg
Sodium	2 mg
Total Carbohydrates	68g
Dietary fibers	9 g
Sugars	44g
Protein	5g

Prepare your juice combining the following ingredients in a juicer/food processor:

- 1 cup of loquats
- 2 cups of cherries
- 1 tsp. of honey

24. Pineapple and Raspberry Juice

Preparation time	5 minutes
Ready time	5 minutes
Serves	1
Serving quantity/unit	556 G / 20 Ounces
Calories	283 Cal
Total Fat	2 g
Cholesterol	0 mg
Sodium	6 mg
Total Carbohydrates	70 g
Dietary fibers	20 g
Sugars	41 g
Protein	5 g

Prepare your juice combining the following ingredients in a juicer/food processor:

- 2 cups of pineapple
- 2 cups of raspberry

25. Guava and Kiwi Juice

Preparation time	5 minutes
Ready time	5 minutes
Serves	1
Serving quantity/unit	530 G /19 Ounces
Calories	316 Cal
Total Fat	4 g
Cholesterol	0 mg
Sodium	13 mg
Total Carbohydrates	70 g
Dietary fibers	22g
Sugars	44 g
Protein	10g

Prepare your juice combining the following ingredients in a juicer/food processor:

- 2 cups of guava
- ¾ cup of kiwi
- ½ tsp. of honey
- 3 ice cubes

26. Watermelon, Guava, and Strawberry Juice with Beetroot

Preparation time	5 minutes
Ready time	5 minutes
Serves	1
Serving quantity/unit	670 G / 24 Ounces
Calories	307 Cal
Total Fat	3 g
Cholesterol	0 mg
Sodium	138 mg
Total Carbohydrates	69g
Dietary fibers	19g
Sugars	48g
Protein	10g

Prepare your juice combining the following ingredients in a juicer/food processor:

- 1 ¼ cups of strawberry
- ¾ cup of cubed watermelon
- 1 ¼ cups of guava
- 1 cup of cubed beetroot

27. Coconut and Apricot Juice

Preparation time	5 minutes
Ready time	5 minutes
Serves	1
Serving quantity/unit	410 G / 14 Ounces
Calories	443 Cal
Total Fat	21g
Cholesterol	0 mg
Sodium	24 mg
Total Carbohydrates	67 g
Dietary fibers	13 g
Sugars	53 g
Protein	6 g

Prepare your juice combining the following ingredients in a juicer/food processor:

- ¾ cup of coconut
- ½ cup of dried apricots,
- 1 cup of fresh apricot
- 3 ice cubes

28. Spinach, Kiwi and Banana Juice

Preparation time	5 minutes
Ready time	5 minutes
Serves	1
Serving quantity/unit	530 G / 19 Ounces
Calories	290 Cal
Total Fat	2g
Cholesterol	0 mg
Sodium	59 mg
Total Carbohydrates	71 g
Dietary fibers	13 g
Sugars	41 g
Protein	6 g

Prepare your juice combining the following ingredients in a juicer/food processor:

- 2 cups of spinach
- 1 ½ cups of kiwi
- ¾ cup of sliced banana
- ¼ cup of chopped apple
- 3 ice cubes

29. Blackberries and Lemon Juice

Preparation time	5 minutes
Ready time	5 minutes
Serves	1
Serving quantity/unit	450 G / 15 Ounces
Calories	273 Cal
Total Fat	2g
Cholesterol	0 mg
Sodium	8 mg
Total Carbohydrates	70 g
Dietary fibers	17 g
Sugars	41 g
Protein	6 g

Prepare your juice combining the following ingredients in a juicer/food processor:

- 2 cups of blackberries
- ½ cup of lemon juice
- ¼ cup of raisins
- ½ tsp. of honey

30. Guava and Melon Juice

Preparation time	5 minutes
Ready time	5 minutes
Serves	1
Serving quantity/unit	600 G / 21 Ounces
Calories	317 Cal
Total Fat	4 g
Cholesterol	0 mg
Sodium	50 mg
Total Carbohydrates	70 g
Dietary fibers	20 g
Sugars	51 g
Protein	11 g

Prepare your juice combining the following ingredients in a juicer/food processor:

- 2 cups of guava
- 1 ¾ cups of cubed melon

31. Melon and Plum Juice

Preparation time	5 minutes
Ready time	5 minutes
Serves	1
Serving quantity/unit	750 G / 26 Ounces
Calories	292 Cal
Total Fat	2g
Cholesterol	0 mg
Sodium	75 mg
Total Carbohydrates	71 g
Dietary fibers	8 g
Sugars	65 g
Protein	6 g

Prepare your juice combining the following ingredients in a juicer/food processor:

- 1 ¾ cups of plum
- 3 cups of cubed melon

32. Raspberries, Blueberries and Peach Juice

Preparation time	5 minutes
Ready time	5 minutes
Serves	1
Serving quantity/unit	560 G / 20 Ounces
Calories	283 Cal
Total Fat	2 g
Cholesterol	0 mg
Sodium	3 mg
Total Carbohydrates	70 g
Dietary fibers	17 g
Sugars	48 g
Protein	5 g

Prepare your juice combining the following ingredients in a juicer/food processor:

- 1 ¼ cups of raspberries
- 1 cup of blueberries
- 1 ½ cups of peach
- 1 tsp. of honey

33. Blackberries and Fig Juice with Strawberry Tea

Preparation time	5 minutes
Ready time	5 minutes
Serves	1
Serving quantity/unit	550 G / 20 Ounces
Calories	289 Cal
Total Fat	2 g
Cholesterol	0 mg
Sodium	10 mg
Total Carbohydrates	70 g
Dietary fibers	22 g
Sugars	46 g
Protein	6g

Prepare your juice combining the following ingredients in a juicer/food processor:

- 2 cups of blackberries
- 1/3 cup of dried figs
- ½ cup of tea prepared with one strawberry flavored tea bag

34. Broccoli, Kiwi and Strawberry Juice

Preparation time	5 minutes
Ready time	5 minutes
Serves	1
Serving quantity/unit	600 G /21 Ounces
Calories	293 Cal
Total Fat	3 g
Cholesterol	0 mg
Sodium	58 mg
Total Carbohydrates	70 g
Dietary fibers	16 g
Sugars	42 g
Protein	7g

Prepare your juice combining the following ingredients in a juicer/food processor:

- ¾ cups of broccoli
- 1 ½ cups of kiwi
- 1 ½ cups of strawberry
- 1 tsp. of honey

35. Pumpkin, Pineapple and Orange Juice

Preparation time	5 minutes
Ready time	5 minutes
Serves	1
Serving quantity/unit	590 G / 21 Ounces
Calories	273 Cal
Total Fat	1 g
Cholesterol	0 mg
Sodium	14 mg
Total Carbohydrates	67 g
Dietary fibers	8 g
Sugars	48 g
Protein	5g

Prepare your juice combining the following ingredients in a juicer/food processor:

- ¾ cup of pumpkin
- 1 cup of pineapple
- 1 cup of fresh orange juice
- 1 tsp. of honey

Exclusive Bonus Download: Crossfit to Drop Fat

Download your bonus, please visit the download link above from your PC or MAC. To open PDF files, visit http://get.adobe.com/reader/ to download the reader if it's not already installed on your PC or Mac. To open ZIP files, you may need to download WinZip from http://www.winzip.com. This download is for PC or Mac ONLY and might not be downloadable to kindle.

CrossFit is the principal strength and conditioning program for many police academies and tactical operations teams, military special operations units, champion martial artists, and hundreds of other elite and professional athletes worldwide.

Inside this ebook you will learn:

- The history of Cross fit training
- What is Cross fit training
- Advice on how to live life to the fullest yet still shred pounds
- Practical advice on the best exercises for cross fit
- The benefits of cross fit training
- Tips to help you succeed
- and more...

Visit the URL above to download this guide and start achieving your weight loss and fitness goals NOW

One Last Thing...

Thank you so much for reading my book. I hope you really liked it. As you probably know, many people look at the reviews on Amazon before they decide to purchase a book. If you liked the book, could you please take a minute to leave a review with your feedback? 60 seconds is all I'm asking for, and it would mean the world to me.

✱✱✱✱✱✱

Books by This Author

The Smoothies for Runners Book

Juices for Runners

Smoothies for Cyclists

Juices for Cyclists

Paleo Diet for Cyclists

Smoothies for Triathletes

Juices for Triathletes

Paleo Diet for Triathletes

<u>Smoothies for Strength</u>

<u>Juices for Strength</u>

<u>Paleo Diet for Strength</u>

<u>Paleo Diet Smoothies for Strength</u>

<u>Smoothies for Golfers</u>

<u>Juices for Golfers</u>

About the Author

Lars Andersen is a sports author, nutritional researcher and fitness enthusiast. In his spare time he participates in competitive running, swimming and cycling events and enjoys hiking with his two border collies.

Lars Andersen

Published by Nordic Standard Publishing

Atlanta, Georgia USA

NORDICSTANDARD
PUBLISHING

Lars Andersen

Images and Cover by Nordic Standard Publishing

11915128R00035

Printed in Great Britain
by Amazon.co.uk, Ltd.,
Marston Gate.